Going for the Grail

Going for the Grail:
A Childhood in Rhyme

Don Gutteridge

First Edition

www.WetInkBooks.com
WetInkBooks@gmail.com

Going for the Grail: A Childhood in Rhyme
by Don Gutteridge

Cover Design – Richard M. Grove
Layout and Design – Richard M. Grove

Typeset in Garamond
Printed and bound in Canada
Distributed world wide by Ingram
 – to set up an account – 1-800-937-0152

Library and Archives Canada Cataloguing in Publication

Title: Going for the grail : a childhood in rhyme / Don Gutteridge.
Names: Gutteridge, Don, 1937- author.
Description: Poems.
Identifiers: Canadiana 20220143366 | ISBN 9781989786611 (softcover)
Classification: LCC PS8513.U85 G65 2022 | DDC C811/.54

Table of Contents

Parnassus

My childhood was as happy
as the grass that hued in green
profusion on Grandfather's lawn
and I spent my days in a
kind of wild beguilement,
grateful to the good gods
who brought me being to this
pastoral precinct, this
passionate Parnassus,
and gave me leave to breed
bardic and ink my world.

Inside

Curly-haired Shirley
doing the can-can
on grandfather's lawn,
strutting her stuff and flinging
her lovely long legs
so high wide and handsome
we burst into prolonged applause
and Shirley grins her little-
girl grin as if
to say, "Seen enough?"
that leaves us singing inside.

Chum

When Marilyn, my chum from school,
in the first bloom of her girl-
hood (with curls as wisped
as winter wheat), sauntered
past the hired hand
and me, the latter thumbed
his crotch, grinned and said,
"Now ain't that a sweet piece!"
and I wondered what part
of her he meant and what
made it sweet.

Legacy

The widow Bray stands
there alone, bee-
deep in her tenderly-groomed
garden (with poppies bleeding
scarlet, roses as red
as a bride's blush and violets
as lush as lavender), watches
the drones, pulsing with pollen,
do their dizzying dance
to apprise the hive of her blossoms'
whereabouts, and thrives
in her flowered bower like a
bloom-inducing wizard
despite the legacy of her loss.

New Bones

When my chum Shirley
grew into her new bones,
the boys on the beach ogled
the rogue swerves and curves
curtailed by her one-piece
suit (too shy
to try their luck, too
boggled to breathe), but I alone
felt my heart hum
like a muted flute when she smiled
at me with a will, as if
to say, "The summer's come
and we are here, two friends
still."

Bonding

My father and I go hunting,
twelve gauges slung
over our arms, ambling
side by side, kicking
at every brush-pile
and bramble bush as the afternoon
wears softly on in hopes
that some prey would startle
and there was no need
for the warmth of words until
a cottontail leaps out
and zigzags away;
"Fire!" and I do, wincing
at the rough recoil, but the rabbit
keeps running and Dad says,
"It's only a rabbit," and I say,
"I'm glad I missed."

Luck

As luck would have it, Bonny
and Sharon agreed to play
"Show me yours" and Bonny
lifted her skirts thigh-
high to expose the puckered
pink rose that lay there
winking up at us,
and when I revealed my stubby
stalk, Sharon said, "Donny,
what do we do now?"
and none of us knew what or how.

Storyteller

For Bob in loving memory

You were my first audience
as we lay side by side
in the comfortable dark, and I
spun my bedtime
dramas about meddlesome rabbits
and bumptious bears, and when
I added voices to my creations,
you murmured, "Ah, that's Bingo,'
or "Oh yes, that must be Peewee,"
and laugh in all the right
places and forgive me my flaws,
and I am so grateful
you made a storyteller out of me
and more so now you are gone
and I still speak into the welcoming
dark and listen for your applause

Time's Tick

On a sun-strummed September
morning we abandon our summer
cocoons and hit the high
road for school, passing
Leckie's farm where Holsteins
graze lazily and shorthorns
remember themselves
and on past Gunn's place
where hogs wallow like hippos
with snouts in the snuffling mud
and the pasture where Grace grips
her stallion with incising thighs
and the hawthorn hedge where this
year's colt burgeons
his brand-new erection
(and the girls blush lushly
and the boys sing inside)
and in the haze ahead
sits the brick-coat
box we will inhabit
until the sprouting of Spring
releases us and I shout
for the sheer joy of titillating
Time's tick.

That's How It's Done

My Dad and I fishing
on Mitchell's Bay, and I watch
in awe at the lazy, lofted
loop of his plug and its soft
plop on the weed-rich
shallow and when a pike
as big as a barnacled barracuda
strikes, he sets the hook
with an infinitesimal tug
and waits for the finned wriggler
to break the surface, its muscling
arc bent like Robin's bow,
defying the grasp of gravity,
but the fight is over, the game
won, and my father grins
at me as if to say,
'That's how it's done!"
and I wish the day would last
forever.

Oval

Under the amber oval
of Mara's lamp and all
along Monck Street,
lavished by moonlight,
we play our ritual game,
and Nancy and I contrive
to share a shimmer of shadow
and for a lucid moment
we do a duo's dance
and I, no Lancelot,
espy a careless thigh
and harbour thoughts of ravishment.

Music of the Muses

I was born with a village in my genes
and the spillage of its sunshine
settled in my soul, and I walked out
each memorable morning
word-perfect and poaching
poems by any means,
the mettle of my mind simmering
with simile and tropes about Cobalt-
blue waters and meadows
suborned by milkweed
and dunes seething with silkened
sand and lilacs breathing
lavender light onto
grandfather's lawn as green
as the glens of Eden, and I grew
anew into each iambic
day, tuned to the music
of the Muses.

Tillage

Each Spring morning
I walk into the wakening world
with the sun haloed on the horizon
above First Bush
and strewing the streets and every
coign and corner with bedizening
light and I wend my way
across the milkweed
meadow below the Bridge
where tender-tipped shoots
upburst from their root
and I stroll along the blue-
hued Lake and its self-
renewing waves and on
past dunes as ancient
as Adam's entry into Eden
and I feel the heave of all
things living and spend
my day purloining poems
from the rich tillage of my home
ground and letting them sing
to my soul.

Long-Ago

With a nod to Michael Ondaatje

I remember the long-ago days
of my youth, when every morning
was a rebirth and we were like
butterflies fluttering free
from their wombed cocoons
in the lucid air over
grandfather's lilac hedge
blooming voluminous and we had
no brink but the blue
embrace of Lake and River
and First Bush where the celibate
sun rose righteous
and I ambled iambic, past
Mara's lamp on is pilgrim
pole, prefacing poems
as I went, to the water's edge,
where I dipped my pen in Ink
Lake and wrote myself whole.

Saw

When Shirley spins the bottle,
I will it to point my way,
praying for the pleasure of a
chaste kiss, but when
our bodies almost meet,
something akin to raw,
unthrottled desire seizes me
sweet and I think of God's
odd look and that old saw:
sin in haste, repent
at leisure.

Vise

Next door to Hendrie's
abandoned coop, a bantam
rooster with his quickening cockade
is harassing his harem, and the girls
decide to play Truth
or Dare and Jo-Anne, forgoing
Truth, announces "The proof
is in the pudding!" and drops
her pants, whetting our wicks,
and we can't take our eyes
off that velvet vise.

As I Walked Out

As I walked out upon
the town that loosed me from the womb
and June enthused the morning
with serenities of sunshine
strumming the streets, and the green
Eden of grandfather's lawn
greeted me outright
and I meandered the village
verges like an Argonaut savouring
the sea and soon found myself
in the milkweed meadow
where tiger-tinted Monarchs
fluttered their two-mooned
wings and nectar-noshing
bees hummed a Polonaisean
tune and I came at last
and always to Canatara
with wavelets lipping the shore-
line intimate and the dunes
stood there as wind-stroked
as the day God uttered,
"Let There Be Light!"
and I opened my iambicized eyes
and the Muses spoke.

Waddle

My Dad on skates: as silken
as a swan mirroring a pond,
and me, just eight,
on my maiden blades, gliding
on my ankles in a desperate effort
to bond with a man I hadn't seen
for five years and more
than one war between us, and I tried
not to notice the surprise
in his eyes, the disbelief
that any son of his could waddle
like a duck on ice and handle
a hockey stick like a dazed
bassoon, and I was grateful
to the gods, whatever their ilk,
who let me wobble beyond
his wounded gaze.

The Silence Between the Stars

In the gloaming over the River
flats (where we sometimes
flew our kites in the big-
breathed wind from the lake),
we played squat-tag
or May I? while the moon
loomed above our random
roaming and threw its mottled
light our way, while we waited
for the sky to darken and ignite
the silence between the stars.

Gran

For my grandmother in loving memory

Whenever I think of you
(and it is more than once
in a new moon), I recall
the aroma of apple pie
adrift on a Sunday morning
or lemon Jello cooling
on the back verandah or a woman
forever aproned, where I burrowed
into a festoon of feathers,
and I remember, too, the lavender
perfume of your quilted bed-
chamber and the click of your change-
purse with a nickel nibbling
my palm, and you and Grandpa
coupled for life, your love
a soothing symmetry, rocking
away a summer's evening
on the side porch, *The Observer*
fluttering at your chin like bride's
bandanna, and I try not to think
about your final face
in that copper coffin,
your smile a grim rictus,
your eyes, that would never glow
again, shut against the world's
will, and me.

Perfection

After Emily Dickinson

Missus Bray spent
each May morning
grazing in her garden among
the flowers she bustled into bloom
to ease the wince of her widow-
hood, and every petal
had to grow just so,
as if perfection were hers
to reach.

Bardic

When I was just young,
I stepped into Spring and the mists
of morning like Adam complicit
with Eden, lustrous with light
(where crocuses bulged in mustard
aarray and tulips bled
as red as a ripened rose
and the earth under them oozed
tubers) and I trod the serene
green of Grandfather's lawn
like Jesus cruising Galilee,
my head swollen Pentecostal
with poems and ribald rhymes,
and I thanked the gods of this
incelibate season and passed
my day: bibbed Bardic
and lost in Paradisal ease.

Joys

In Grandfather's yard
I said a welcome to crocuses
in their labial lustre
and tulips dipped in menstrual
red and lilies lit
with swallowed light and rose-
buds in tumescent fettle
and wild iris with nettled
stamens and pistoning pistils
and in the eaves above
starlings remarked on the merits
of the day and sparrows gossiped
on the gables and it was all
my delight to sit me down
and compose a poem to celebrate
the urgent surges of such
a Spring and the joys it leaves
unbroken.

Untugged

I was almost twelve before
I ventured into the big beyond
that squeezed my village and kept me
hugging home all
those incubating years,
where I grew in wombed degrees
and let the poems percolate
from Foster's Pond or the sands
of Canatara, and I felt like Jesus
ambling easy on Galilee,
my head singing biblical
with psalms and Parnassian parables
and I was content to remain
there, untuggd by Time
like a fly in amber, the ink
of my childhood drying
on the page.

Riches

When I was a boy in breeches,
I stepped out into the misted
morning and said "Hello"
to Spring, when buds nudged
and Grandma's tulips ripped
airward and bled beauty,
and forsythia, scissored by sun,
bloomed anyway, and I walked
upon the town like Adam
aroused in Eden, rinsed
in innocence, miming his Maker
and pressing every edible
object into the pincers of a poem –
rupturing reason and begetting
bedlam, and I've known
since that paradisal day
that my life would abound
with the riches of rhyme.

Rhapsody

My village re-imagines itself
each morning when the sun
rises over First Bush
where robins rhapsodize
and the streets and alleys, etched
in the muscle of my memory, throb
with mist-mellowed light
and I greet them like Adam
dreaming in Eden's perpetual
day and I wend my way
iambic to Canatara's rapturous
sands where on-shore
breezes blow like the breath
of a loose-limbed bellows
and rustle the silken curls
of the sea-grasses and I want
 to capture such passing home-
grown mementoes in the rhymed
crucible of a poem.

Cribbed

Miss McDonald made
a writer out of me,
praising the story I'd cribbed
from the class Reader, but the words
were all mine, rising
from some liberated nub
inside like a dew-winged
bird, unfazed
by the perils of the page or the rigours
of rhyme, and I swallowed Parnassus
whole, knowing even
then that poetry is the soul
singing to itself.

Derby

My pal Wiz confected
a go-cart out of orange
crates and abandoned buggy-
wheels, and I pushed him
up and down the town,
pausing to accept the polite
applause of bystanders,
and when Herbie Gilbert
rolled past in his Tin
Lizzie, he saluted us
with his ooga-ooga horn
and we felt like born-again
winners in the Soap-Box
Derby.

Solo

I saw her there but once
and that was more than enough:
Marybelle Cooper
curled on the sun-strummed
sands of Canatara
in her one-piece suit,
clinging to her girlish curves
like a lover's ruffling hands,
and I spent the rest of my day
humming without pause
like Orpheus on his lute, and singing
solo to Cupid's apt
applause.

Gleam

When Jo-Anne dropped her panties
and exposed the prize between
her thighs, she had a gleam
in her eye like Delilah's snipping
Samson's lofty locks,
like Salome's doing her death-
dance unfrocked,
like Bathsheba's dithering David,
or like Eve's outwitting Adam
with an ample apple, and what
I want to know is did they
enjoy the triumph of their titillation?

Elapse

Marybelle Cooper,
my best friend's cousin,
stood behind the white
picket fence that hugged
our yard in her Tartan sweater
under which her just—
about breasts breathed
serenely, and when she smiled
my way, all the sonnets
I longed to sing lapsed
on my lips and when she smiled
again, something tugged me
aside and I knew for the first
time what love was.

Dance

When evening came down
upon our village, we ran
headlong into the gloaming
to play our home-grown
ritual games, and in season
and out and fancy-free,
we found new reasons
to rhyme, and like any other
Medieval town, we also
danced and kept our time.

Chime

Shirley doing the can-can
under the Parisian trees
on grandfather's lawn:
all soothing thighs
and nubile knees and,
aiming to please with a
glint in her eye like Eve's
ogling the apple, she chimes:
"I lift my leg so high
you can see my cherry
pie ai ai!"
and we all wake up
in China.

Tropes

I was told the first word
I uttered was "No!", as if
I were warning the world of my arrival
and wouldn't take "no"
for an answer, a one-word
poem in hopes of establishing
my bona fides, and soon
I got the knack of nouns,
the vim of verbs and the rigour
of rhyme, and these were the tropes
a poet could drown in.

Ghosts

Everywhere I look in the
noonday dazzle or under
the slow moon of a summer
evening, I see the ghosts
of those who touched and left
their tender trace: my grand-
father who lived for three
years in the trenches and then
lived again and Gran
aglow in the smiles of the littl'uns
tugging her apron and Uncle
Potsy who loved me until
I grew to love him and my Dad
who skated as smooth as a swan
polishing a pond, whom
I forgave the itch of his addiction
and a host of others: boy-
hood chums and village
vassals who peopled my life
and imperfect poems, who let me
hug the world home.

Green and Growing

If it's Spring in the Point,
the lilacs on grandfather's
hedge are livid with light
and there is bulb-burst
and fledgling fusion and juiced
buds anointed in the sun's
nuzzle, and I find myself
meandering the milkweed meadow
with a thirst for everything green
and growing, and the air aloft
is soft with the singing of larks
and the drone of home-going
bees, and I have such a
longing to pull the perfect
poem out of blood and bone.

Gardens

In the milkweed meadow
a stone's throw from grand-
father's yard in the sizzle
of summer, butterflies flutter
at ease on the afternoon breeze,
bees, peregrinating
from flower to flower, nosh
on nectar and, high above,
a lark soars with song,
and I am welcomed into
this paradisal place
as one of the Elect, and I pull
open a plump pod
with its silken secret like Jesus
breaking bread before
the Apostles, and I say a prayer
to the god who fashioned such
gardens for our innocent use.

Silver Spoon

Contrary to popular view,
my grandfather held
his knife in the left hand
and his fork in the other,
and just free from my silver
spoon, I took to cutlery
like a duck to a reed-rife
pond, with left-hand-
knife and right hand-
fork, and oddly enough
we soon grew fond.

Enraptured

When I was young enough
to know better, my world
was hedged by grandfather's
lilacs, lavish in morning
light, and an arbor hung
with roses, and I roamed the village
beyond like Adam idling
in Eden or an ardent Argo,
welcomed by the sea-warm
womb of an archipelago
until I met the edge
of the everywhere I called
home, free from Time's
tyranny and happy as a poet
enraptured by rhyme.

Easter: At Nine

On Easter morning, we polished
our shoes till our souls
shone through, donned
our fresh apparel and sallied
off to Sunday School,
where I dreamed of Jesus, pinioned
on Golgotha like a
lepidopterist's specimen,
entombed in the Devil's dark
and, calling on the heft of Heaven,
rolled the stone away,
hobnobbed on the road to Emmaus
and, to the prolonged applause
of the Apostles and hoisted by helium,
rose resplendent to Paradise.

Biblical

The sun rose over
First Bush each
summer morning like an
old-testament prophet,
like Elijah and his chariot of fire,
and I was Bible-bred,
teething on its stories: Adam
ungrieving in Eden,
David and his potent pebble,
Moses cleaving the Red Sea,
Samson with his liberated locks
(his eyes gouged out on Gaza),
Daniel flouting lions
in their den and Zacharias
trembling in his tree,
waiting for the Messiah, and my mind
seethed with such Promethean
parables (as I weighed the wages
of sin) and I grew a story-
grammar I'll pursue until
my last poem perishes
on the page.

Celibate

Each summer morning
the sun boiled out of
First Bush and lashed
my village with lacquered light,
and I greeted its streets like Adam
poaching Paradise and rousted
Butch and Bones and Wiz
to reconnoitre every ell
and alley, all the way
to my boyhood beach, where,
at last, and to no-one's surprise,
I found myself alone
and celibate: with an itch for history
and a passion for poetry.

Bolt

They say that lightning never
strikes the same tree
twice, but in the summer
when I was almost me,
both of the maples that hugged
grandfather's house
and shaded my boyhood
games were struck down
by a single savage bolt,
and the home where I was lavished
by love and jolted with joy
and which I spun into a
dozen pulsing poems
and ringing rhymes, stood
there shivering in the sunshine
like a prude nude, and I knew
then that nothing is ever
the same again.

Forge

O the gorgeous girls of Canatara
in their one-piece suits,
curled on the sizzling sand
with their brand-new breasts
and the tender tuck between
their thighs while the bashful boys,
lashed by lust in the forge
of their desire, try their luck,
eyes upon the puckered prize,
saluting the day their God
bi-gendered the world.

Glance

O Nancy Mara, you were
the belle of Canatara!
I see you still in your blue
one-piece suit,
seducing those Saharan
sands with your lithe-limbed
beauty, and later on
stroking the bevelled swells
of our mutual Lake with silken
symmetry, and I would forgo
my share of the world's luck
for a single glance meant
just for me (and enough
pluck to return it).

Daughters

When I was young enough
to know better and still
in the gist of boyhood, I looked
at the girls around me with a
particular interest:
Nancy Mara to whom I took
an immaculate fancy;
Shirley McCord with her high-
stepping strut between
teasing twirls of baton;
Grace Leckie, two
rows over with breasts
breathing through wool;
Judy Hammond waving
Hello with a long-legged lope;
and Marybelle Cooper,
the girl next door
who lit the wick of my desire:
Daughters of Eve one
and all, who took the fall
for mankind and the insights
of an apple and the illicit pleasures
of conjugal joy.

Thorns

Each summer morn,
across the street, I follow
the straw bonnet of the Widow
Bray floating above
her flawless flowers in a
bee-buffed breeze,
and she seems pleased with the
garden she grows to ease
the grip of her grief, knowing
full well that every
rose has thorns.

Stuck

I never put much truck
in girls until one of them
harpooned my heart, and I loved
Maybelle from afar
like Romeo his Juliet, marooned
on a balcony, and I gazed at the
white-picket fence
upon which she preened
pristinely, and at the supple
swelling where I dreamt her new-
minted breasts slept,
and I longed to pledge my troth
like Lancelot his lady, but my tongue
tripped on itself, and stuck.

Squeeze

The Reverend Bell assured us
God so loved the world
He gave us His only begotten
Son, but I had other
thoughts: girls with tender
breasts, and smiles that made
my loins loiter in their throbbing
sockets, and hockey games
where I, improbably, scored
the winning goal, awed
by the elixir of applause, and so
it was I did my best
to squeeze Jesus into my heathen
heart.

Mooch

My dog Moochie rhymed
with pooch, a water spaniel
with webbed feet and no
pool to paddle in,
who assailed passing autos
as if he could bark them to death,
who followed me to school
as if I were the Pied Piper,
where he mooched his lunch on the
front steps, and when
he fell mortally ill,
my father drove him to the
countryside and dropped him
there, alone and intestate,
and I wondered if he might
have met someone
who loved dogs more than
the cost of a vet.

Galleon

For Grace Leckie

I dithered by the wayside,
waiting for Grace to ride by
on her roan stallion, her prized
thighs gripping its gallop,
and when she deigned to wave,
my heart went striding apace,
and I felt like a chuffed buccaneer
counting gold on his galleon.

Fledgling

If it was a Saturday you'd find
us in the aging Imperial
where we sat enthralled by the
latest six-gun mayhem
of Hoppy or Johnny Mack
in their sagebrush sagas,
clinging to a cliff's edge
as the Cavalry arrived in the flick
of a minute to vanquish the ululating
Indians, and hissing whenever
our hero kissed the schoolmarm,
and soon the cartoon would come
catapulting in technicolour
onto the silver screen that magnified
our fantasies and stoked us with stories
any fledgling writer
would die for.

Local

Whenever I think of the Point,
I imagine a place that drew me
full-blooded into the world,
where poems grew fantastical
on trees made lyrical
by light, where budding bards
could fletch and fly and be
anointed laureate of the local,
groomed for greatness, and where
home was its own season.

Spare Parts

O Nancy Mara, you broke
my heart before I knew
what true romance was,
and, like Abelard, I loved from afar,
as chaste as Eloise in her nunnery,
and I might have been the one
if only I had spoken my love,
but my tongue was tied when
your gliding glances stunned
my spare parts.

Truce

We dubbed her Juicy Joyce
before we knew a thing
about the gentle gender
or what aspect of her anatomy
we had in mind (and whether
it was tough or tender), but when
I passed her in the litter
of her yard, I did my best
to be kind and keep my eyes
averted from the bud between
her thighs, and when my mates
gave voice to their mocking moniker,
I demurred, and called for a truce.

Soothed

Grandfather's yard was all
my world when I was young
enough to know better:
with a lawn as looming as a lake
and two tall trees
where sunlight lived
in the breeze-licked leaves
and lilacs hung dozing
in droops and honey-bees
noshed on nectar where lilies
bloomed in petalled puffs
and snowdrops teemed
hectic in the hedges that hugged
my world home, and when
I tired of innocence, I lay me
down and soothed myself
with bardic dreams.

Bid

The Widow Bray bid
"Good monring" to her flowers
and moved among her daffodils
and daisies like Gaia garnishing
her humble Greek garden,
and won the praise of half
the town for her Green Thumb
and countless hours lived
amid things that grew
anew whenever touched
by her taut, untarnished hand

Bellow

In Sunday School we sang
of Jesus bidding us shine
and God's spared sparrow
and the little light we let
live in our small corner
and thine, and we rang the rafters
raw, our voices swollen
with the Holy Ghost
and a hatful of Hallelujahs,
and I wanted to come to attention,
salute and bellow "Rule Britannia"!

Our Team

In Sunday School we were told
that Our Saviour suffered us
to come unto Him, that the Lord's
house had many mansions,
and when the organ wheezed out
The Doxology, our voices went soaring
to the beams above, for we were
certain we were on the Jesus
team.

Date

Shirley doing the fan-
dance on Grandfather's lawn,
showing a curve of calf
and an intimate inch of thigh,
twirling her mother's boa
and shaking her garden gate,
as if she were old enough
to be billing and cooing
and we had nerve enough
to ask her for a date.

What is More

Summer was the season strung
between June and September
when we were young enough
to be free and combed
the sun-thumbed streets
for stray empties loitering
in nooks and crannies, whose
two-penny return
would buy us a grab-bag
or a brace of gumballs,
and we lazed away amber
afternoons on Canatara's
heat-seizing sands
and dove for bottle-caps
in our blue-bellied lake
and compared shy erections
in the boys' change-room
with its spy-dy hole and took
no guff from anyone
elder than us, well-meaning
or goitered, for we were easy
in our bones and, what is more,
immortal.

Undaunted

The houses of my youth haunt me
still, like the debris of my dreams
or shadows clinging to the shapes
they once made: *Mara's*
place where the roof slumped
as if too weary to sit
erect above a porch
where Gerry's Dad took
a last fall from;
Bryant's bungalow with its
manically manicured lawn
that withered when his hectic heart
exploded; *Barker's* shack
that welcomed in the Winter
wind and seething summer;
Hendries squalid colony,
each piece unpoached
by paint; *Bradley's* quaint
cottage where missus and mister
dreamed in their dotage;
the shambles of *Lumley's* shanty
in a yard where toddlers
drifted, and Grandfather's house
where I grew greening in my bardic
bones and joined in the impossible
pursuit of the perfect word:
undaunted.

Wordless

Missus Bradley, sunny
weather or not, stood
on her front stoop and un-
tethered a wordless cry,
heard in every nook
and cranny of the town and,
like a bee without its buzz,
wondered who she was.

Meme

Point Edward: July 2018

My village lies in quiet
collusion with the sun, long
shadows lean lengthwise
from houses that held me hostage
for a dozen seasons, and streets
my feet read like a bard's
Braille, sit just as
they did when I roamed them
like LaSalle on a sortie, combing
for news of a better world,
and the Bridge still skewers
the sky and Mara's roof
still tilts as it did
when Jerry and I swam
our summers away in the Lake
as big and as blue as the Baltic,
with dunes a-doze in the hectic
noontide light, and the school
where I scribbled the first
line of an interminable epic
is now gone under the wrecker's
ball, and I am as reluctant
to leave this meme of memory
as a bride her epithalamium
or a groom his darling's garland.

Bauble

When I was young enough
to know better, the grass
on Grandfather's lawn
had the sheen of Eden on it,
and the hedges that hugged me whole
bloomed numinous: hung
lavendered with lilacs,
and I combed those holy
grounds and the dappled shade
of the Manitoba maples,
unfettered and glowing easy
in my bones, and, like Adam,
rinsed in innocence and paradisal
light, I bedaubed whatever
I met with natural nouns
and voluptuous verbs, and all
passed peacefully in my greened
garden until, from the edge of
Everything, I heard someone
calling my name and urging me
on to the brink of Beyond,
where an apple winked like a
bright bauble on the Knowing
Tree, and I seized it with a
wordless fury.

Clinch

Shirley was the first girl
no longer to be just
a pal, and I watched in awe
as she bloomed like a slow rose
in a lash of light, and when
she smiled my way, my tongue
hummed and hawed as I tried
not to ogle the fresh bevels
of her body or day-dream
a libidinous clinch,
for I knew even then
that somewhere the Earth
had moved an inch on its axis.

Lonely

For Tom in living memory

You were a May-day lad,
born just as Spring
sprouted, when the soil teemed
with seed, released by rain
with the ease of April in it,
and a sun a-boil on any
horizon, and shoots, as pristine
as the preening paddocks of Eden,
bloom tumescent, lusting
after light and its livid
lash – and this was the promise
you brought to the morning of your world
as you grew greening into your bones
and looked for ways of loving
and put the majesty of your mind
in play, but somewhere in the
second act, you nodded
to polite applause, bowed
to the grinning gods, and vanished,
and now I cannot gaze at a
tulip cleaving in the brave
blurt of its bulb, or lilacs
lush with lavender or a daffodil's
saffron dance without
the thought of your lonely going,
leaving me in the grip of a grief
that festers like flesh ripped raw.

Phalanx

When Granny Reeve died,
I remember the golden
gladioli from Mrs. Bray's
groomed garden and a casket
buried in bloom from her pied
bower, which seemed to ease
our grieving, and I thought
of Granny being carried
to Heaven on a phalanx
of flowers.

Immaculate

When I woke up in the womb,
I had no urge to leave
its amniotic ease
or brave a muscled tunnel,
but rather seemed content
to hearken to a heartbeat
and its soothing lullaby, but some-
thing deeper and more dire
thrusted me into the ambience
of an alien air, where I uttered
"I am," and all our days
since have been spent finding
a way back to that
immaculate room.

Awakening

The sun rises over
First Bush, the lava
of its light like the slow
opening of a June rose,
lacquering the leafage
and rousting robins from their
yellow-beaked sleep,
setting butterflies a-flutter
in the breath of a breeze and then
anointing a village by a Lake
with its lucid layering before
seeping agleam into alleys
and ells, and there on a
sun-strummed street
stands a boy something
like me, navigating the day's
breaking, a-dream with desire,
waiting once again
for the world's awakening.

Hide and Seek

Under a night-sky
starved of stars with a moon
pruned to a sliver of silver
uneclipsed by cloud,
we loiter aloud below
the amber oval of Mara's
lamp, darting into the
larcenous dark just
to let the shiver of it
whet the appetite, and soon
we are cloaked in shadow and slyly
gendered (our hopes erotic):
lips nipping lips, a palm
impatient upon an unintended
knee, but the "All free!"
like the cry from a goitered
throat, draws us, still
seeking, back to the lambent
ligature of Mara's light.

Pierian

Every poet prays for a
Pierian Spring, a place
where poems abrupt, whole
and unthrottled by thought
or any notion other than
saying the unsayable,
and mine was the Milkweed Meadow
where Grandfather's lawn
gave up its green preening
and I could find an elfin
air more suited to the self
I kept estranged and muted
and where I could be at home
in my bardic bones and let
my soul sing.

Bachelor

I wandered the milkweed meadow
like a bachelor bard looking
for something bridal to teethe on,
debouching pouches to learn
their silken secret and letting them
flutter on the breeze like new-
hatched butterflies, drunk
on their own delight, and soon,
like a moon-soothed horizon,
I felt the soft surge
of words batten on my breathing
and I turned them inside out.

Leila

Leila Burgess, without
breaking a sweat, spawned
a dozen younglings because
she couldn't curb the kind
of urges that begin begetting,
and she earned her bread and butter
by scrubbing her neighbour's floors
and dreaming of the days she set
a dozen hearts aflutter.

Bellicose

It was an extraordinary morning
when the sun bloomed over
First Bush and the streets
of my town were laminated with light,
and I burst from my growing abode
like a bellicose bard looking for
something to indict
with the words welling up
in tight-fisted frenzies,
and I wanted to grip the gist
of all things "village"
and put them in the pulsing pentameters
of a poem that would last until
the crack of the doomsday gun.

Nurture

When I was young and lilacs
hung in lavender loops
and rosebuds nudged
and tulips, once a-dream
in the dark, erupted, and honey-
bees nibbled on nectar
and robins let a song
throb in their throats, I made
my way deep into the
milkweed meadow
where new-sprung leaves
slept in the noonday's
lacquering light, and butterflies
unbuttoned on the breeze,
and it was there I found
a tongue to say the words
I almost knew and nurtured
the knack of using them.

Nothing to Say

Missus Bradley talked
to the walls, but they had nothing
to say, so she tried her luck
awhile on the front porch,
but the evening breeze brought
no news of this,
that or the other, and so
she had to be satisfied
with whatever the hum in her head
said.

Saunter

On her way to the grocery
my Gran takes a leisurely
walk one block north
where Mrs. Hart waits
to have a chat about this
or that, and coming back,
she saunters one block south
where she and Mrs. Shaw
take stock of the day's
doings, and then my Gran
and her tightly-bunched bags
cross the road, arriving
home in time for lunch.

Bred to Be

I was bred to be a bard
in a town that seethed with similes:
the grass on Grandfather's lawn
was a green as the glens of Eden,
lilacs on our hedge drooped
in fruitful loops, our maple-shade
was as dappled as a Mackintosh,
milkweed pods were as puckered
as a bridegroom's lips,
their silken insides as soft
as the down on a hatchling's breast,
our lake was as blue as the jut
of a jay's wing – and these
were the seeds of my heathen verse,
and I let them breed in me
until they were ready to be
flung gratuitous to the young
gods of the universe.

A Little Like Me

My grandfather survived
three years and a half
of terror in the trenches, with blood
and mud commingled amid
the crude blooming of bombs
and the shudder of shells shivering
the air above the empty acre
of no-man's-land,
where men, wrenched from everything
holy, perished for King
and Country, and I wonder if he found
a slow moment to dream
of coming home, hale
and free, to father sons
and grandsons, one of whom
might have looked a little
like me.

Holy

My Gran was chary of churching
but she tithed Anglican just
in case, and observed the Sabbath
by thinking of her maker as she kneaded
dough and scythed apples
for the pies she offered to those
she loved most, and I
was ever the first to sample
the merchandise, remembering
to thank the Father, the Son
and the Holy Ghost.

Limned

O Marybelle Cooper! You were the
first girl to stir
something burrowed within,
and I see you still, limned
by morning light, in your tartan
jacket, where brand-new
breasts slept in silken
repose, and when you deigned
to grant me a smile, my heart
did cartwheels and the farmer
denounced his dell.

Pastoral

When I was a budding five,
Grandfather's lawn
rolled before me like the
ocean God gave to Noah
and his ark with its bellyful of beasts
or, when the sun simmered on it,
the Sea of Galilee that Jesus
sauntered his sandals on,
and the hedges that held the waters in
were lissome with lilacs that drooped
in languid loops, and further,
where islands idled, a brace
of maple trees, brushed
lush by a teasing breeze
and below that belled umbrella
grasses danced in dappled
delirium, and I was young
enough to float freely
in my bones, and roamed these
pastoral desmesnes as if
they were hearth and home

Bejewelled

I was weaned on Bible stories:
Adam and Eve cavorting
in the Garden, naughtily nude,
but, alas, raddled by an adder;
Delilah, lopping hubby's
locks and cheering as the temple
columns toppled; David
and the potent pebble that felled
a giant; Daniel at ease
in the lion's den; Moses
in the bulrushes, tucked in wicker,
then commandeering Commandments,
weathering a wilderness and cleaving
a sea; Elijah, chuffed
with God and cruising moonward;
Zacharias in his trembling
tree, loved by the Lord;
and Jesus galivanting on Galilee,
dishing out loaves and fishes
and pinned on Golgotha like a
mutilated moth: and these
were the tales that fuelled my fancy,
gave me a grammar of plots
and protagonists with which
to bejewel my world.

Remembrance

In the Point we called our cenotaph
simply "The Monument," and etched
in stolid stone were the names
of long-ago battles
too brutal to be celebrated,
and on the slim plinth
a roll-call of those
who gave their all for the king
of a far country, and atop
this edifice of remembrance
the bust of an unknown soldier
stares out over the town,
looking lonely and unanointed.

The Knack

Into a May morning
and the village that spawned me
where the sun rose over
First Bush like a blown
bloom and lacquered the streets
with a soothing luminosity,
I strode – like Adam greeting
God at the gates of Eden,
my body a womb for words
and their slow explosions, my head
a-burst with bardic dreams,
and I plumbed the tillage of my town
for the prescience of a poem
or the knowing flow of an ode,
certain I was born with the knack.

Festooned

Missus Bray dreamed
of blooms in her garden,
festooned with flowers of every
ilk, and when the sun
came up, it soothed
the day's bouquets as soft
as any satin or silk,
and she bid them bask in the
purview of her praise,
and when night came down,
she dreamed again of daisies
and daffodils in their delight
and let her widowed heart
teem.

Budding

As I grazed the Parnassian pastures
of Grandfather's lawn,
I was pursued by bardic dreams,
my head agog with an extravagance
of stanzas and rhymes looking for the
chime of a couplet and rhythms
that dithered and danced, and I wanted
to ink the world and its people
in passionate pentameters
to amaze and delight: my words
unbudding, liberated by light.

O What a Morning

O what a marvel is a summer
morn in the place where I was born,
when the sun blossomed above
First Bush like an over-
exposed rose and lacquered
the streets with lyrical light,
and I, sequestered in my home-
cocoon, set out
to harvest happiness in the dappled
shade of elm and oak
where infant breezes whelmed,
my head agog with bardic
bravado in quest of the perfect
phrase to amplify the iambic
dance of this daunting day,
pleased to let it fester
like a bruise in the bone before it
brightens and blooms.

Woo

Whenever we caught a pair
of dogs 'doing it' on the walk,
the girls blushed as pink
as a peony, and we just marvelled
at the conjugal apparatus
of canine wooing and dreamed
one day that we too
might give it a go – gratis.

Cradle

I've been told that even as a
toddler I was often whelmed
by an upwelling of words,
nurtured by the sing-song
thrum of the nursery rhyme
and the three-pronged plots
of Goldilocks, imprudent pigs
and Billy Goats gruff
enough to enfever my polyglot
fancy, and I sensed even then
that poems were bred out of bone
and the body in the ease of its breathing:
our lilting, infant syllables
unquelled in the cradle.

A-Dazzle

When I was young enough
to unremember, my world
was composed of Grandfather's
yard, hemmed in by hedges
where lilacs hung in lavender
loops and roses swooned
on the arch of their arbour, and each
bloom sunned itself
singular, each petal
its own proud poem,
and something instinct
in the breeze trembling between
the leaves brought me up-
right to the brink of seeing:
and all was then a-dazzle.

Lost

Missus Bradley stood
on her front stoop, blinked
the sun's ink from her eyes
and uttered a cry that blossomed
from her bones and soared up
through the throttle of her throat
and out to the furthest ear
in the titillated town, and there was
the shudder of shame in it
and a yearning for something
smitten she had long-ago
lost.

Far to Go

On this Summer's day
an hour before the dark
devours it, my lake is as blue
as the Heaven that holds it
and we swim gingerly into the
soft surround, our bodies
thin-skinned, bloodless
with buoyancy, unhinged
from its hunger, and way out
where the heat-haze hovers,
a sun hesitates on the horizon
like a moon too bruised to fall,
and we know we all have far
to go.

Kingdom Come

We had only one murder
in the Point, in the years where I grew
bemused: young Lumley,
beguiled by the girl next door,
already betrothed to another,
refused to take her no
for an answer and, despite
a tumult of tears, girded
his loins, borrowed his brother's
gun and blew her brains
to Kingdom Come.

Author Biographical Note:

Don Gutteridge was born in Sarnia and raised in the nearby village of Point Edward. He taught High School English for seven years, later becoming a Professor in the Faculty of Education at Western University, where he is now Professor Emeritus. He is the author of more than seventy books: poetry, fiction and scholarly works in pedagogical theory and practice. He has published twenty-two novels, including the twelve-volume Marc Edwards mystery series, and forty books of poetry, one of which, Coppermine, was short-listed for the 1973 Governor-General's Award. In 1970 he won the UWO President's Medal for the best periodical poem of that year, "Death at Quebec."

Don lives in London, Ontario.

Email address: dongutteridge37@gmail.com.